Gerry Loose

Printed on Water

new & selected poems

*for Ingrid
with best wishes!
Gerry Loose
CCA Nov '07*

Shearsman Books

in association with Mariscat Press

First published in the United Kingdom in 2007 by
Shearsman Books Ltd
58 Velwell Road
Exeter EX4 4LD

in association with Mariscat Press, 10 Bell Place, Edinburgh EH3 5HT.

www.shearsman.com

ISBN-13 978-1-905700-07-3

ISBN-10 1-905700-07-5

Copyright © Gerry Loose, 2007.
Introduction copyright © Peter Manson, 2007.
Cover image copyright © Morven Gregor, 2007.

The right of Gerry Loose to be identified as the author of this work, and of Peter Manson to be identified as the author of the Introduction, has been asserted by them in accordance with the Copyrights, Designs and Patents Act of 1988. All rights reserved. No part of this publication may be reproduced, stored in a retrieval system, transmitted in any form or by any means, electronic, mechanical, photocopying, recording or otherwise, without the prior permission of the publisher.

Acknowledgements
Some parts of this book have previously appeared in the following magazines: *island, Object Permanence, Urthona* and *West Coast Magazine*; in the anthologies: *Hours, Fifty Lines Written For David Connearn At Fifty, New Writing Scotland* numbers 13, 20 and 22; Radio Scotland (and for which what can be read into a thing was a National Poetry Day commission); the websites: *Interpoetry, Scottish Poetry Library,* & the collections: *a measure, Eitgal* (Mariscat Press), *The Elementary Particles* and *Tongues of Stone*.

The publisher gratefully acknowledges financial assistance
from Arts Council England.

Printed on Water

Also by Gerry Loose

Change (images by K. Sweeney McGee)
Yuga Night (with Larry Butler & Kathleen McGee)
Knockariddera
a measure
Eitgal
Being Time
The Elementary Particles
Tongues of Stone

as editor

The Holistic Handbook

as editor & translator

The Botanical Basho (with Yushin Toda)

Contents

Full Powers:
    An introduction by Peter Manson   7

The Gateless Gate	10
Eitgal	15
even in this city	32
songs of commerce	33
rain and how we choose	38
days	39
strange	40
The slow	41
where is the clang	42
the facts of the matter	43
happy to be on Kelly's roof	44
the martial arts	45
The herb garden	49
There are some words that I dropped . . .	50
Stachys betonica	51
rose	52
Holy Loch Soap	53
daughter	70
son	71
for Sam	72
from: a measure	73
two commentaries	79
four commentaries	83
speech has no title	89
anything a symbol	90
what you gave me	92
spell for the untimely dead	93
first naming of the island birds	94
the island in September	95
from: synchronicities	96
sometimes the weight is equal to . . .	98
even elegant mind is clinging . . .	99
A belated & random birthday greeting	100

a valentine for Morven   101
discussing herons   102
for Larry in the Western Infirmary 261104   105
what can be read into a thing   106
from the ogham
    Cloghane Carhane   108
    Cloghane Carhane   110
    Poltalloch   111
    Dunadd   112
    Keiss Bay   113
    Moor of Carden   114
    Gigha   115
    Inverurie   116
    Abernethy   117
    T'yn y Wlad   118
    Cunningsburgh   119
    Gurness Broch   120
from Stroke Mother   121
what a tight membrane   138
from the deer path to my door   139

jottings   143

Full Powers

This collection of Gerry Loose's poetry selects from thirty years of work. Loose's writing is always, in the best sense — that of poets as different as Louis Zukofsky and Ted Berrigan — occasional. We orient ourselves in it by means of shared, often dateable, landmarks: the birth, growth and crises of children and of crucial personal relationships, the politics of the Cold War and of more recent state-sponsored disenfranchisement, the ageing and passing of parents. Though references to practice are usually left implicit in this poetry, the thirty years saw Loose's centre of attention change[1] from Zen to Tibetan Buddhism, which this non-Buddhist might try to characterise as a shift away from a focus on the Void[2] to one which includes the Plenitude which is implied within it. One of the pleasures of knowing Gerry is sharing in the exhilaration of his engagement with the minutest details of the living and non-living worlds (worlds I think we've both become less confident of distinguishing between as we get older), and the tendency of these details to branch off towards boundless complexity before our eyes[3]. Uniquely, Loose unites a Linnaean intoxication with names with a poet's critical sense of the limits of Language and of naming as a process of setting limits, whether on boundary-stones marked in Ogham or in the restrictions placed on human potential by military euphemism. That Loose can combine his sense of the particular with an equally clear-eyed view of the larger dimensions of landscape, history and ethics makes him a valued, wise and above all useful friend (I can barely see further than my own nose), and makes these poems — detailed on every scale — a varifocal lens for twenty-first century eyes.

Peter Manson
October 2006

[1] 'Change' is the title of a matrix-game based on the *Book of Changes*, designed by Loose in collaboration with Kate Sweeney McGee and published as a boxed set of 64 cards by Bob Cobbing's Writers Forum in 1987.

[2] The Artist Yves Klein once exhibited an empty, white-painted gallery space under the title 'Le Vide'. Albert Camus' entry in the visitor's book read "With the void, full powers". A year later, Klein's friend Arman crammed the same space so full of objects that no human could enter it, naming the result 'Le Plein'.

[3] The first conversation I ever had with Gerry was at the height of my own fascination with fractals. I remember writing down the equation behind the Mandelbrot Set, which Gerry recognised from its use in the mathematical modelling of animal population dynamics.

that it should be starting when appearing finished

when finished all should be starting and appearing

& that all is appearance and nothing is ever begun

The Gateless Gate

I

The grazed knee of the mountain
the water, rain
sodden skin of earth washed-off
six acres to pile against the dyke, land slide
six acres of sheep dreams.

Listening to the radio
waves over, through the mountains
like fathers
heads cocked to the wooden cabinet
cloth speaker
Hilversum, Motala
crackle of tongues
rain squalling music music.

Floating woodworm dust
from the rafters
an empty land
a gate protecting
nothing from more
nothing, con-
joining death

2

now, the rain falling
now the sea calling me
now with the sycamore pips falling here seeding
now with my soaked sleeves spinning
now tumbling and rolling down wet from birth wet to
death into descent
now descending dropping falling to seed nothing, now
now, now, pivoting
on a fear taut belly long down now
now here now

what choice is there but to sing *death*
what choice is there but to sing
what choice is there but to love
what choice is there but to chant
what choice is there but to hate *all my days*
what choice is there but to dance
what choice is there but to dance *this dance*
what choice is there but to dance *this dance I dance*
what choice is there but to dance *this song I sing dance*
what choice is there but to dance *this dance dancing me*
what choice is there but to dance *this dance through me*
what choice is there but to dance

now

3

Death played in the haggard
and waited for the old men
of the village.

He was three years old, blond
his young eye was cunning
and one gaffer had the milky eye of cataracts
gravely, he was told good day.

When Death fell in a fit
the drunk old man
sleeper in ditches, bent
to the hailstones
one lung gone, farmlands drunk
kidney raddled, managed
a clear eyed look.

And when Death rode the donkey
of the last old man, after gangrene
crept along his skinny old man leg
and the surgeon sawed it off
there was no offspring
but Death.

Along the dykes
the fence stakes cut from willow
shot out green leaves.

4

The tadpole ghosts
will not leave us.
Gaping mouths
reddened guts
flouted through opaque bloated bellies
they mouth bubbles
will not become
won't metamorphose
still hungry for our watery life
in the sloughs.

5

Dogger, Fisher, German Bight
Valentia
ice rims the western edge
visibility twenty miles.
How to describe the indescribable:
goldfinch on the limb
take the things closest
record them, draw the line
the outline
you have the shape.
Someone will make a container
by stamping dance
whenever you open it it's there
it's replenished
you look you see
pay the dancer please.

Eitgal

Part One

1

Am I not Eitgal   winged fury   wings of wind
the blusterer   the breathmaker   the singer
the scalder
fletch of Michael   a feather fallen of the
archangel   plume and pennant of Skellig
of Michael   abbot of this sea rock where I am
blown   where I blow
ach a windbag
Christ abate my pride

2

Wordblind half bard
soured cleric
unchaste monk
succoured futile flesh-stone

3

Are those to the east
the mountains of my youth
passed through for Skellig westward
scald crow hill cloud shadows taking
days to pass   black wings on the
greying rock   lichen shadows   growing
on the flanks of mountains
neither slower nor quicker
than moss than black birds than my faith
the passage of a cloud shadow

4

Notice then how the sun petrifies
the night wet stones   the sea's waves
melt to pudding   my questions borne
down   doubts flattened
felicity in prayer rising
gannet heavy   to fall smack in the sea
leave me staring stupid
work to be done

5

Moan of monkish prayer doleful introspective
to sing christ in sun days gale days alike
lifting old stones moss stones
with worksong unbidden to the lip
tuneless and tuneful unthought
and thick with now rising over head and ears
as our cells   stone on stone
swell and diminish as the work
laborare est orare

6

These things I see   I miss   to bend the knee
flying spiders on the wind making that leap
I cannot   peregrinatio   on umbilical abdominal
web line   landing anywhere   unknown stone or
campion grove

Small boys chatter   unknowing
words in the face of   god
a choir   falling apart   a looseness in the face
flying   of stiffness

7

If the Caolcu   the holy men   the whippet
thin men of Iona   those doves of the church
Colm's darlings   returned here

these silly monks blow me up
seal fed   grain fed   sheltered
yet complain

flutter at them   not at me. Learn
hardship from the north.

Perhaps he serves neighbour best who is not hungry
christ's men   we all are
sin to please the flesh
they pleasure themselves mortifying

8

Eitgal is a quern
wordquern   grind corn   grating men host thin
sacrament   monks for the sacrament of love

I know Mary   **I know Mary**

I wear the monks for her
I thresh I grind quern-Eitgal for love
love of the earth
love of the mother
the mother of god

9

Eitgal wants a woman
quiescent member tumescent menhir
rock hard rocked into menhir socket
erected with ropes hauled into
soft earth moist mother
exposed to weather
hail flailed crack of lightning

ah the horned god wears my meat.

The brothers get by not loving
some of the brothers desiring
Eitgal   loves all
Eitgal wants a soft woman human
no harm in that   where's the harm in that
harm to Eitgal
cut it off cut it off

10

Poor pale wrinkled fishskin dead fingers
digging wet moss
my tongue too like this back to the root
(cleft foot   sounding board palate cloven)
wormlike bloodless
sooner than glib

11

Whey faced lank haired clerks
in the hermitries and father houses
herons   bent over illumination
trilling of larks and linnets
rather far a fat fish fed sea goose
to stave off unsought starvation
the better to prayer

12

Pig latin   pork latin
watery snot ridden phlegm
we grunt and snuffle
hawk over our prayers   fatten
out the lean latin
we ate belly of pork
nipples intact on the singed scalded skin.
Pigs

13

The night moth   turning aside
stunned by daylight
resting here under this green
by night seeking the sun that terrifies
in weak rushlight
we sing singed by the awful vision
eyes filmed   sancte venite
candles to the dawn

Saille   little willow   chieftain tree
hawk tree   spring tree

                        come to me Mary
                        christ come to me

wind whirl   turn   roll   ear shell   volute   whirl

                        come to me now

sallow   wallow   will shroud   corpse mouth bubble

                        come Mary   christ

sally   leap   spring back   resilient salvation

                        come now

crack willow   withy   goat willow   sally
white willow   sallow with ears

                        come to me Mary
                        christ come to me

Part Two

15

Starlight through the cell door.
What is Eitgal?   Ten stone animal
aspirant
                    ant
on a floating leaf wandering to the edge
and the edge   and back
waving arms upwards   craning   peering
seeking rescue.
Rustic reciter of strange litanies
mediator   parenthesis among men
animal plodding a perishing wet stone
yet I give thanks

16

Creeping on the crust of this scar
burrowing into the skin
seven sorts of snails   I have counted
and me
I shrive   shrivel slowly in salt spume
I'm growing old I grow less bold
marrow dries   tinkling shell
back pack   heavy
my humpy house.

It's not all feast and fast
slow and slimy silvery trails we leave
where others live the world
day by day we steal eggs
crawling the cliffs
the gulls shriek norse   berserk.
Brittle armoured worms

unpalatable slugs
are we not to be saved
ora pro nobis

17

To the alter prosator   Blathmac of Ia
listen   we're local lads
gael and gall of these islands
Eitgal   Darerca   Brendan
Gerald   Kentigern   Uigbald
charity begins here

Fools perched on little stones in the sea
we squabble for muck
though I hold this earth dear
these pebbles
Skellig   Iona   Colonsay   Aran
Mull and Man
Lindisfarne and Ultima Thule
Hy Brasil and the Orkneys
Alba   Banba   Anglia   Northumbria
are muck without

May god forgive us
we try

Part Three

18

The light creeps crepuscular up the walls
always at sea in my unmoving boat
fragments of an old dream recurring
will I be that old man
no hairs on my legs
mumble   become a murmurer
mime and dance my words
for you   you smile behind hands and
backs   I giggle twist and dip
who laughs last
the light creeps up the walls
listen

19

Failbhe had deformed feet
and stood for no nonsense.
Bending the knee
to Felim the king
his lumpy left pediment
peeped out from his hem.
God   the ugliest foot west
of Egypt   said Felim
God is good   I bet   said Failbhe
there is one as ugly much closer
this looking Felim straight in the eye
the king (the king) swore and rose and bet
Failbhe rose too and
pushed forward
his other crab foot.
It was hard to keep a straight face

20

Failbhe clumb down the cleft for dulse
and picked bushels from the strand.
I took my ease above   bees drowsing me
when rounding the ness come the Danes.

Failbhe shoulders a sackful
and creeps and crabs back
up the rift while they
beach then pound across sand
to clatter off the cliff.

Aah. As a man when he first hears
the cuckoo   Failbhe cocks his head
upends the sack on him below
who falls back on his bum
streaming sea weed while Failbhe
pensively slams him with scree.

Coward come down
gobbles the blear eyed dunce
Failbhe garlands himself with weed
jigs and capers   shakes his tool
coward   come up   come up
Failbhe   miles Christi.   Soldier of Christ

21

Believe me
dropping blood is easy
compared with the horrors
of place
going into the unknown

never again to speak my tongue
to see my folk   hear
the coughing of cattle
in the stall of dawn.
Red martyrdom takes
only foolhardiness   courage
takes only conviction   strength.
For exile   going into the
whiteness
you must know the face of god

22

Finian   on this lake island
this testing ground bound by rules toil worn
we are austere   as novices we try hard
to do without fear
for that is to deny faith
we do without sadness
because that is usually self pity

praying   we stand
in cold water like trout   it cleanses us
sleeping   we roost
on rocky ledges like peregrines   it lightens the load

we do without music
though we growl our psalms
we do without meat
though we spice our greens with sorrel
willingly we do without bread
though we crack teeth on stony oats

but Finian   brother   storekeeper
must we also go without beer ?

23

Sluicing down
The rain cannot stop.
Inside for three days
grey days
black prayer
stones above
stare at the page
stare at the wall
the page won't hold
the hand is the letter E gone mad

then wakened by light   a strange dog scattering hens
the sun among the clouds   splintered in a thousand
still puddles on the hillside across the valley
spiked and magnified in the drop left on each tasty
looking willow bud   a land rinsed clean

At the door
scrimshanks
arms akimbo
shaven poll
now hear Eitgal's patter stop
the Word   re made

24

Failbhe   Patrick   and myself
came to an island.
We had vowed
(among other things)
silence   save once each
every seven years.

After seven of them   I
was sick of lumpy porage
and said so.
Seven years later that sourpuss
Paddy   told me to
make it myself
and another seven years passed.
It's high time (said Failbhe
after 21 years in that place)
you two stopped arguing

25

When I asked Failbhe
how big was heaven
what was the size of it
Round about the same size
as the inside of your skull
was his reply

26

Do you hear me
my heart my life
half of my soul
the way is hard
and I want to be
ringed by creation
not negation

do you hear me out there
the other side the glass
rapping tapping

the prison of my days
tit to pit
hear the bubbles
the fish mouthings of my faith

do you hear me
crying from my desert
life   life   love
you asked a word
I answer you
if you hear me
stay away

27

A boss came
scratching his head
and told us
of arguments
among his men
about work about war
about when about how
about who about why
about horses about hounds

Failbhe's eyes widened
Are you still alive
go back to your office
tell yourself
you've been
dead a year

28

Another day   with
blood-mote grasses
in heaping wind swell

come here I want you
said Failbhe
we'll have a good argument now
like other people
(did I ever tell you
his eyes were blue)
you're some dog aren't you
but you are a dog
you can't best me can you top that

in all fairness now
what could I say to the man
but he's right
You're right Failbhe
you're right of course

we knocked back the beer
looked out to sea

29

Failbhe groaned
all the virtues
are here now   by me
except one   the
one I should live by

so I walked into it
and asked him what

oh misery   he groaned
that a man should
always be mocking
himself

30

A thief came in
with a knife
Failbhe said
No bell   it's tolled
no book   it's read
no gold
please take the bread
the bedclothes the
pen   ink   satchel
I only have nothing
you can't take it
I can't give it
it's already yours but
I would like
to pass it on

31

One day
at last and of course
Failbhe went away
and there was still
work to be finished
if only dreams
though I wept

to think he would never
see the slow green leaves
tongueing spring
this physical temporal
green we eat
with all our senses and heart
that he sorely loved

and the cat pined
and I move to not
think

32

Failbhe walking one day
came across a severed head
which he toed.
Wearily   yellow eyed   it spoke

Look for nothing
twelve hundred years from now
it will be heard and found strange
and the sound
put in the mouths of others.
Always be a free man when you speak
not a slave.
Abolish the rich.
I have forgotten
what my words mean

even in this city
the whoop of a gull

I'm breathlessly climbing pavement
there at the top of Douglas Street
that instant the freed eye
and to the south   the hills
and behind   the hills

the equally rare sightings
of myself

songs of commerce

1

my eyebrows grew long in the mountains
now I hang about in town
tending shop   11am   1990

> *is this you opening or closing*
> *I'm a clam already*
> *how much is the buddha*
> *you don't accept credit cards*

I listen to the traffic   the telephone rings
can't Access Gautama   no Visa for the Way
what kind of deal is this

2

he wears a jumper and glasses
she wears glasses
looking for a chest of drawers
georgian if it can be found
at the right price
I don't have one but
I'm polite
they're smiling I'm smiling we're smiling
if I wanted I could be in New York or wet Galway
I count my bills
I try to abandon cleverness

3

I hear on the radio that spring has arrived
moving away from the particular
the exact shape and colour
of cut leaved cranesbill   bloody cranesbill
that grew in my wall
pigeons murmur unasked in my head
billing (as they say) cooing (as they say)

here and now in this shop
like crested grebes like aerobatic ravens
we agree to certain rituals
to certain necessary compromise
to the appropriate noises
courting customers   a human exchange is made
just there   see: the creative.

A benediction –
may my customers go forth and multiply

4

because everything can be turned to one use
sunlight fills the glass
time is money   money is power
power corrupts   time corrupts
I sit here in the cliché
I sit here in the stereotype
what else turns (I sit here in the gallery)
sit here and walk the byways
thanking her

thanking him for spending
glad to be left alone
obsequious lying shopkeeper
this is the Way

5

money of course destroys the brain
it's a well known fact
tonight I'll buy more wine   how glorious
to drink   drunk   in the groves of south Glasgow
roll up   roll up   I need money
for pomegranates
for a lunar eclipse
for rain far out on the Atlantic fishing for mackerel

6

palm wine cups   a sperm whale   a fertility figure with erection
a firespitter   a carved leper   banana trees   benares brass
shiva   ashanti stool   hausa gourd   senufo masks
medicine boxes   buddhas   ducks   frogs   wayang golek
fake tang horses   batiks   lombok bags   stone heads   bronze heads
no one buying

saturday evening I taste brass
who fed me these words
that I spew them out undigested
misrepresenting what the saxophone says
how much I mistrust all this

7

I sit around waiting for the next century to arrive
not too seriously
a collision among the strange bipeds
who inhabit the future
who waits for history
meanwhile back here the leper leers on one leg
the africans are making strange silent noises
the shoplight is rain and safety
if I was an amputee I would still love you

8

ten ways to lose a customer

as my martial arts teacher
was fond of saying
number one : don't be there

       (I had a wooden duck for sale
       a customer asked the price
       when I told him he said
       can you knock something off
       only the beak   I replied)

       a customer asked the price
       of a carving
       fifty-five pounds I told him
       can you do a better price he asked
       sixty pounds I said is a better price)

if I must be there
nine ways   quick   quick   try

selling blasphemy   selling rainbows   selling dreams
selling the mist on the sea
selling the frost on the mountain path
selling bitterness   selling nightmares   selling silence
selling the cinema in my head

rain and how we choose
the weather here in the valley

the mountains pass bearing
the purple swollen sexual

wound of the copse of birch
the hillside gives birth to

creatures   we lumber past
all we'll ever need

days

drawn in

the watering can
upside down

against the

rain

strange
a moment

in darkness
a noise of

small rain.
To hold this

The slow
rise of

the bird in
the instant

before
landing.

where is the clang
of this spade on stone

where is the fruit of the tree
that made this shaft

where is the fire and rod that made
beads of weld on this steel

I stole the soft mist
it was mine always

I stole the air from the wind
it never knew

I stole the heron's gaze
she had fished enough

tell me : what can I take,
what cannot be taken

the facts of the matter

making a song for myself
in cutting wood on a clear day

goldcrest working the haws
brown wren in her quickset cave

Sweeney in the icy tree
perhaps seeding this one

and the sudden worm
in crumbling wood shocking

pink and funny
as a grinning dog's cock

so close
to being sawn off

the song the worm
laid aside

made for a slower fire
than the wood

happy to be on Kelly's roof

last night drinking tea
the whisky long gone
weighing words

this morning on the roof
eyeballs dancing
in the iron heat

seeing south
top of the ladder
five thousand acres of bog

remote holdings
silent days
a long way from the poets

the martial arts

I

the things we cling to
it's easy to give away

the things the troubles
the small compassion

it floats away : jetsam
the gulls squabble over.

friendship arises and
finds me empty handed

the river runs deep
under my car

again I pretend to move
from here to there.

the knife slices
once   twice

to whom shall I
give the present

of my death

2

like my light eyed girl
like my dark eyed boy

a man singing
in the emptiness

pruning words
to fit only silence

there is something
offered for each

moment each half
moment in joy

the roar of moonlight
in the hills

3

working hard
twenty four hours

the whisky tastes
just like whisky

if I could only make out
those motes in your eyes

what would be gained
what lost what changed

something lifted me
to the top of the mountain

and left me there
it's uphill work now

listen we don't know
what love is

4

already beaten
with a stopped mind

never to be seen
never shown

deep inside
the small child waits.

and what can ever
be said

in tension in ease
a stutter a stumble

between the word and
nothing lies the poem.

cutting the cackle
of course

once more breaking
the surface here

soft wind   small rain

The herb garden

I'm not sure if it is at all possible to steal stones but I took them anyway from the fields and from the ruined houses of the townland, anywhere so long as they were the right shape and size, hefting them through rushes and briars where the barrow would not go. Two or three feet long and no more than ten inches wide; ideal were fallen lintels from doors, better still from windows.

I buried them half in half out the stony soil like a small Karnak two feet out from the south facing wall, filling the pocket with our building rubble mixed with black friable soil you could eat : the riches of aeons of rock, generations of leaf mould, lifetimes of dung.

The herb garden I made there interested me less than what grew wild in the wall – the tiny ferns sheltering dinosaur insects and the scarlet cranesbill cutleafed and bloody. And the clump of campion I stole from Sceilg Mhichil.

I claim treasure trove on this cairn – the capstone prised back – filling still with drifting dust motes

There are some words that I dropped in the slow and squally summer meadow I was renting from Kelly to make hay.

Walking the windrows with my hay pike   nothing over my head only the clouds   a two day old telegram was delivered there to me : my father was dying.

I stuck the pike into the flank of the hillside   dropped the words and travelled four hundred filial miles.

Old words – a wisp of hay that a nourished cow already ruminating will moistly so gently nuzzle like a lover's kiss   the wisp in a corner of the manger   the manger in a cow cabin that has remained unchanged undisturbed for an entire generation.

Words I had thought once to digest and cud into a poem of the year my father died   of the year my second son was conceived   of singing land dreams.

Who will chance upon that abandoned half song on the edge of that meadow in lost 1978   a distant parish at the lip of the Atlantic?

Stachys betonica

then I find the words are there
were there all along
lodged in cracks
behind clumps
behind grasses
where shield bugs row their legs
upside down

where my small daughter
pulls weeds with me
weeds   insects   words
black earth sticks
to our fingers

I aimed for this moment
unswervingly   unknowingly
through the tangle of bishopweed
through the various orders of insects
through the gaps between

rose

there are poisons which would
keep me alive longer
in delicious agony
the rose spreads through my veins
parasitic   not the colour alone
but the wooden stem veins
thorns chafing within the rose
is a rose   and not
beautiful   nor is it beautiful
has no beauty   is

change alone blossoms beauty
as the rose buds flowers and dies
change moves
I read of the dead of Babi Yar
30 000 in one trench alone
pin down that dead insect word
that rose red carapace   beauty
change
if not this   then nothing

Holy Loch Soap

1030090487

I

    i

steam bath water lapping me your silk skin
how I sing of for you mammalian siren song

motor cars break covert rocket
away from bushes traffic lights

pistons and big valve snare
the jazz drummer in my chest cavity

beached and dripping winged fish my lungs
my lung fish flutter flute and sing

this air is too thin to carry
my breath words gasp and die I lie

    ii

if I could only love money
could I earn love woo it
fickle neon eyelashes lowered
on off on off belisha courtship

    iii

bank managers cut discs of realpolitik
I drift in regurgitated oceans of wine
I climb shrinkwrapped buttered mountains
my melting matterhorn shames night hawks
insider dynasties founder on and on
responsibility rattles my newspaper tears

iv

at thirty nine I can tell
popes to come clean
blood does not wait for answers
on good days I nearly understand

v

how can I ask for your epitaph
trident compensation

sitka christmas all across the high lands
mickle wishing well coins muckle banked

sterling eyes and pluribus tongues
how can I ask for your epitaph

vi

grandchildren of my father
might understand why my tongue
treats her to poverty you say

is it time will you count me now

kettles boil and telephones ring
pall bearers approach
benedictine commonwealth night falls

vii

I set the scene for you
something akin to a proverb hatches
in cockroach cracks
Pope's men explode
Diet of ants
Arms deal signpost
Kiss Me Kate

2   0800100487

Holy Loch   (Loch Striven   Loch Ewe
Machrihanish   Stornoway   Cape Wrath
Thurso Forss   Thurso West Murkle   Tain
Inverbevie   Edzell   Rosyth)

USS Proteus
USS Hunley
USS Simon Lake
USS Canopus
USS Holland
USS Hunley
USS Simon Lake
      the ships

Waggle o' the Kilt
      the show on the promenade

3   0915100487

action replay truncheons integrity
in time we will arrive

your colour prints smile mother
father large child small child dog smile

US navy designer moustaches
ungay jive circumflex mouths

smiling milled edge defender
of the faith defend us into death

4   1147100487

professionally processed
there is no military occupation
navy blue discharged from the spectrum

processed and printed
leukaemic alcoholic figments
we also accept dollars

I have no negatives handy
I would like reprints and enlargements
have a nice day

5   1330100487

boom da boom across the steppes
comes uncle's moustache now
the commissary is suspect

pavlov's fairy world domination party
bring your own bottle
underbed drawers a feature

refusenik intellectual subplot
this is unbalanced
the rest is censored

6   1530110487

genuineness ectoplasm
verbal with nonverbal
tone of voice with content
nonverbal with nonverbal
content with word connotations
black brogues with white
trenchcoat surgical smile
salt lake city salt
lake minder eyes
latter day saints
I infer that is a swollen gland
under the armpit can I infer
the millenium
no the ball mists over

7

I'm a bad jive bear
I know the handshakes
man

what's happening man
yeah I smoke a little dope
yeah

a little budweiser
commissary vodka
ok

joined after Nam
stayed on
right

defend the free world
gotta do
pint of that tartan

me I accept
bathroom full
personal responsibility

8   1355120487

holy loch of the soap
the poor of a nation
to worship I consume
cracker barrel honky tonk honky
wobbling globes of shower flesh
around sphincter enthusiasts
iron pumping head bands
one two one two sweat
dollar droppings scramble
oh clean cut lubrication
collision love violation
ligament featherlite action packed
holy loch assumption spent
consummation cindy
sunshine reverie

9   1500120487

on the other hand
rhyme I understand

no holy loch conspiracy
no US navy heresy

father hear my confession
peace is my profession

i

here in my bathtub peeping
a submersible on the firth
diogenes or aristotle
I admit ignorance ambivalence
is this self pity form
a lack of naked courage
dialectic self disclosure accretion
my nose flattened against the window
of cake shop america
even my visa
to font holy loch expiring
I try to come clean

ii

my observation is we
bottle and sell the sun
outbid and liquidate
the long stolen journey

iii

I talk to you from far away
it is doubtful you hear
your indifference tells me
in other places
mockery is a crime
I am probably grateful no

I am properly grateful
what stories do
nagasaki hearth crickets
tell their grandchildren

    iv

meanwhile back at the ranch
I tie myself in knots
call words ideas
hispid lipped they know better
yang the triple bar branding iron
slithers to the bunkhouse
where I lie with night
where I am night
trapped in words
confessional distortion
verbs splinter proof
where I am night accused
unmentionable
moustache of silent villainy
dawn knives gleam
I write swiftly *the*
pen is mightier than

sister jasmin
palmist reader adviser
resolver of all problems
I am gifted to help all
I also lift all evil and illness

one visit will convince you
that is the true Holy Woman
also speaks spanish
flat 3 3rd floor

you are a family man
your loved ones are far away
there is water
you are charitable open handed
you like to watch tv paint in oils
but you have many enemies
regulations follow you
stop you having fun
you are often bored
you like a drop or two
there is much unhappiness
I see a blinding flash
I see much something something
you accept responsibility
for personal hygiene
thank you dear

so I goes
suzanne's a lovely mover
that's what a man is
porn photo shame
gay kicked out in spy base scare
maggie comforts hero

you can be breaking up
a fight and get busted

our troops test red missiles
wake up now to the jap cunning
leftie MP backs libya
you can be breaking up

you got a drink problem

13   1345180487

respect
listen to what others say. attend. do not interrupt.
own your own views opinions statements.
explicitly ask others about their opinions or views especially
in circumstances where there is a strong consensus in one direction.
explicitly recognize paraphrase or empathize with others' views
or opinions especially if such views are different than yours.
acknowledging a person's ideas and allowing space for views
does not necessarily mean agreeing.

respect
the evidence bikini atoll 1954 white powder afterwards
falls on beaches and people (news bulletin: savages) of
Rongelap and Utirik

respect
the exercise holy loch this year this man says if he felt the need
he would beat the shit out of me would he test fallout on
Colonsay and Tiree

respect
specific things that lower the respect score are
interrupting others before they have finished.
telling others what to do feel or think especially if they have

not asked for advice. the respect score will be lower if the
trainer hears in your voice tone that you are telling the other
person what they should do.
rescuing others, that is, attempting to explain person a's behaviour
or statement so other group members might change their attention
toward person a. refraining from sharing feedback with another
person under the illusion that it will hurt the other person.

glendaruel glen of the
river running red
of columbine and bishopweed
of the rowan oak and alder
of the cup marked stones
of kilbridemor and kilmodan
ardacheranmor where I talk
in the sun with friends
the mewling buzzard cartwheels
as though the black jet
       like a falling mountain
         that blackly travels ahead of the exploding air
       as fast as my thought
never was
the curlew bubbles and whoops
and the cockerel crows
and the cuckoo
and the echo

where I enter the lyrical
on a need to know basis

Titan   Atlas   Thor   Navaho   Snark
Nike-Zeus   Mace   Bear -A
Shyster   Scud   Blinder   Sark
Nike-X   Blackjack-A
Griffon   Henhouse   Looking Glass   Skybolt

15   1640060587

the eleven prophecies of st columba

studio A : Bambi
studio B : Rambo
Virginia Blue Ridge
New England Patriots
Carolina Tarheels
New Hampshire Live Free or Die
St Augustine Alligator Farm Florida
Christmas Island H-bomb Tests 1957-8
Love thy neighbour but don't get caught
God Bless our (mortgaged) Home
Expect a Miracle

16   0945110587

it's all serene as
we communicate we plot

loose change I attempt to
maintain change I examine

my naval america
america is here there

is a precise boundary
hopscotch america scotland

when we grew up and stopped seeking america america
sought us out and established a frontier trading post
we are all indians now and I try to maintain change
but my personal stress management includes nicotine
I puff addiction firewater a cigar store indian woodenly I
my intertribal sign language is lost in the
exchange rate the jargon of self growth at any cost
compassion and everything has fallen to democracy the last
hope democracy the clever agent of self suppression
we are all dead in defence of our rights to
suppress ourselves thank you lone ranger
quién no sabe lone star for allowing me to oppress myself

17   1450130587
                                                        (2055170687)

    what brings you to holy loch
    a californian woman is asking me

(through the window tenderly passes
a platoon of poseidon submarines)

        like a thrush whose cockerel song it is said
        is a split atom of territorial imperatives

(large peaked male baseball caps
drift above other passersby as ritual

headgear of shinto priests moving
into religious timeless other fusion)

since the arcane handshakes of money
the alchemical reduction of yin and yank

since the secret of cost effective alcohol
are among the things my father did not teach me

listen let me ask (you in
the middle of next week or) what

brings you to holy loch

18   1545030687

Flying Fulmar
Thunderer
Point Spencer
Storm Petrel
mv Juno
USS Lafayette
USS Los Alamos

during loading
and discharging
adjust ship's
or shore ramps
to allow slack
in lazy links

in the hall marked chain it costs
to train a nuclear warhead handler
that handler is an investment
so that he does not fall apart show no return
I help him relieve his tension stress
   tv dreams all your needs in our shop
   corsets dresses uniforms shoes wigs etc catalogue £4
my pay cheque is smaller than
there is no slack

19   2100170687

time organizes and categorizes
in zones of morality
headstone all facts
any newspaper is a ballad
time headlines lyrics
in marshalling yards
in zones of morals
hallo sailor
it won't go away

20   1630180687

time was
when it was all simple
ferns unrolled
outside my old cottage door
umbelliferae I could not name

rosa gallica
bells of columbine
and foxglove
geraniums everywhere
the wild kind
willow herb
all nodded in my direction
I must have been their height
no not childhood
this last flowering explosion
and time disintegrates
numb I wait for new movement
where are the emissaries
the blue flies buzz and batter
at the window
where are the agents of change
who is dreaming me now

daughter

for Biddy, 8
she does not realize yet

with the full of moon   the ocean
due west to Newfoundland
humps its back
an old dog on a bone

bares Moher teeth
coral teeth   Clifden teeth
Clew   Clare   and Achill teeth
to empty Blacksod sockets

flow, tides
my own daughter's smile
solid as only the sea
singing moon

as moon resembles moon
as moon replaces moon
she passes on

bones   I am here
with her shining face
in the rock pool
on the curling dog Atlantic lip

Na Forbacha
Galway

son

for Kian, 18
he does not remember yet

how cleanly we step into air

    cattle file across
    the hump of hill I climb
    to watch Arran float
    below nimbus
    this single place

this we know
we have realised together
sinister things mount the finger now
we misconceive
from our world abuse
we hallucinate
them they
batter the insides
of our eyelids

the wheel rolls onto us
as we dream of purpose
as if there is a purpose of dreams
as if this is the purpose
as if affirming clear air
as if air existed
as if we could hold it
fill our lungs
& speak

Auchincruive
Ayr

for Sam

but from the gut   lends of memory
killing chickens in Kilmackerin   goat kids   or fishing on Valentia
   in tongue/d intestine

but from the gut   only questions as babies ask   mama
tree tractor bus   later affirmations   become separations

son   my son   a question may also be a lament   of passage
[how you held my hand   across roads   //   when small
gutsong of lives in memory]

a prayer to the animals
my still warm viscera   handled   metastasis   each day arrives
each   night arrives and I lay down   die and wake up and carry on

but from the gut   what words   to send now   to help
you cross roads   along roads   [where once you took my hand
on the back of a winged bull   an eagle   two dogs biting their own
tails]

but from the gut   fronting heart   paraphrasing intestines
nothing satisfies   let it stand   for now   21st December 1996
a complete icebow   spectrum around the moon   also forgotten

a palpitating small thing   who speaks now   the small bird of
sense is shot down   you   for her decorative angel wing
you   are dumb your eyes   books   2am trash
cigarettes wine brandy weed love

I can say this

from: a measure

damn any lover
that comes near you

let her mound wither
let her sweet lips crack
o let her cunt wither

damn any lover
that comes near you

let him wilt   impotent
let him be numb   castrate
whatever his eternal sex

o christ &
in my fifth decade   &
an obsidian heart

yet reading love poems
signs   omens
breath soughing from me

for your true caress

hold love hold

your nipples are
not flowers that can be picked
& fade
they are nipples
they are not mine

your eyes
softening with a light
half understood
looking past me
these are not mine

your lips and tongue
softness   parting
not mine
though I want
to be in you   be you

I do not own your
soft belly   (though I know it well
I do not own your
thighs   (though I can feel them
your surge & swell
your vortex
are not mine

        under the roof   under stars
        tongue become stone
        the midnight bin lorry
        bellowing outside is
        my night   my love

        not caressing   not possessing
        the night is mine
        black as the pits of your eyes
        mine is a hole
        in my belly

because I knew you would be there when I woke
because of the way sun slanted through dust through trees
because flies then cleaned their legs
because cars pulled away at junctions
because people died
because I died
because of the hives of bees
because of the sea at Ballinskelligs
because of soft rain
because you spoke the name of my dream
because dreams acted me
because you slept & dreamed me awake
because there are dreams
I called you lover
        & your silence loud in my ears
        the glance of your eyes a mirror to my grasp
        my grasp at moonlight
        my fingers grasping love

we rose
from the hill
beast headed

        and I entered her dream   she said
        and with a thin tube blew
        and blew into her mouth
        and into her nose
        and blew into her ears
        and she struggled
        and I blew

trying on wolf & dog & crow
trying snake & fetish & bull
horse & bison   we rose

& love was left behind
small parcel
it is

    we cannot articulate   singular
    we cannot say   fewer than 2
    verbs decline extravagantly starting *we*
    thou is we   we say

                & the word came down
                like a slave from above

    pushing upward
    becomes enthusiasm
    becomes the snake
    becomes a rope trick
    opens the heart
    becomes our will   *we*
    are rising to meet
    the word
    defining love

    & sun & moon head south
    while we sing   sing   sing
    & where is love then

triune   we hold up the stars   hags
a three sided figure   multiplied

                                                           demons
drawing in stars with our cunts
& a cock fountain of stars   eyes

            a tongue on night sweat skin   tongues
            the pressure of my lover's leg

                                                         neptune
impaled on the trident of human hospitality
where the start of love is kindness   adrift

diversity is love's manifesto   unmaking
love manifest

                                                     assumptions
                    where breath draws the snake
                    & the fish heart (fucking) gasps   unassumed

unmoving but moved   resolutions
the moon under water

                                                     unresolved
as ever does not hold
stars or hearts   (mists)

                       broken in love   unrevealing
                       or mended in

                                                        depth
the threefold way of love
kindness   humility   & a flowering   teeming

which blossoms metaphors   ghosts
skies & stars

                    which we uphold with
                    where

two commentaries

\# 1
the creative gives possession in great measure gives
the creative fourfold gives possession in great measure
gives the principle in principio erat verbum
heaven gives fire gives heaven
sky gives lightning
cold gives sun
the active the strong & the firm gives to the beautiful
the depending the clinging
father gives to the middle daughter gives to the father

& so the wheel continues

\# 2
the power of the great   (is to)
decrease its power
looking for the unnameable
in all innocence   (expecting the unexpected)
influencing
arousing

thunder comes

trying hard to
feed my pain
that it will slow

become fat
forget me

in the morning my
stained tongue

a whisky shaped hole
in blood red brain

a shaped reverie
in which I am spooned out
scared to rise

love has moved
I remain

You will never
switch me off.

Together we grappled
sycamores the sinking earth
and yes the
phosphorescence of Waterville bay

voltage arced
spitting the
kind of truth
curlews & owls
recognise   peeled
willow wands of
a kind of innocence
mute deadnettles
dread   we

came through charged
carapaces opening
never to not
walk darkened hillsides
on Oughtiv's thigh

in all this shining
blackness you
will never switch me off.

what amity is.
here. sojourning.
wandering. travelling.
dispersing then
                    that horse on
                    the hill top. my
                    great crying out
polarizing
                    all directions meet
always here
not then never when.

enough.

what amity is
from me straight
through this paper
to you

four commentaries

1 : *she*

opens her mouth
swallows pearls   spits entrails

diviner of that her own song
she sings a water bird
she sings riches in the house

a silt black field
silently consents
to hold one crop

three mountain peaks
tell her her heart is true
that words are speech

swarming insects
that speech is not needed
that time   is

2 :   *foot & calf resting*

two boulders in the park
where I smoke
possessing directed going

& crumbling structure
house walls   eaves
books   games   white

goods   we open the
fridge & there is love
left over   enough

for one park smoke
boulder   smoke
a going dance

3 : *invocation*

Handel returning that
mandrake root of memory

not to trust to
question questioning

to doubt doubt
as crosslegged she

watches movement resolve
to dots across

her screen eyes
ombra mai fu

the moon has fallen
in the river again

seeds   shirts   anything else
is on my shopping list

4 : *his*

body repeatedly steps
behind his mouth   reaching

to walk say new pastures
and yes say it   pray

when he steps on toes   tails
he must go on straight hearted

stepping around   mouthing
strange smelling words

go on with the heart   argue
go with the heart

through steaming new grass
through

until standstill   where it is
proper to hang the sun in the sky

if he only sees
however long it takes

earth continues
its belief in heartbeats   in mouths

: *becoming open heart text*

going directly behind meaning   mouthing water crystals
exchanging interlocking alphabets   ice cube letters tinkling
in the glass   flesh sticking to frozen metal

where there is an eye above everyone who stands designed on
the ground   women men and dogs   even herds of deer
coming together   coexisting   limpets to each barnacled rock

where alphabets vault beams   wear wings   put on hats
undress   on ground of their own choosing

sourcing the head   which whispers deities   urgently whispers
obedience to the heart   warns of birds with clipped wings
sitting where alphabets congeal   having fallen

remembering the morning wind rolling in from the Atlantic
laden with grey rain

as the bee stings it is done

& yes death kissed me full   on the lips   teeth   & yes I tried on
his diamanté shoes   & yes found him wanting   & yes
his drum kit did   not move my feet

she did   she does but   after her is a little death   whose arrogance
drinks with butchers

though time has its own kinesis working its own field   stable
extended   flexible   pliant   a tender city I move over the

line.   I'm leaving mythologies   I only put on wings
to please   & my hooves don't please

it's enough to rattle   my rib cage   click my fingers   dance
my own earthspan dance   unzipped from throat to groin

an ear of corn   an apple falling   a rib removed   I no longer
talk in tongues

speech has no title

(word alone cannot open, she said.
Samye Ling 190797)

the sound of syllables
    the om   ah   hung
& the sound of the circular saw
    tearing the tree off into planks

it skims the water it bobs tail
    on rock its flesh insight
muscle tissue syllable
    the hundred syllable

anything a symbol
for anything else

the bedroom mirror is emptiness
the chain it hangs by attachment
to causality

anything is also only
itself but also its not-self

there is pain behind the
humour in your eyes or
is it the other way round

you glance away and
like a lighthouse shifting

beam in a stormful night
illuminate other craft
mirror more empty rocks

before your gaze light turns
full circle on its high

and lonely gimbal maybe
I'll have foundered on
the not-rocks certainly

will have moved
making emblems of

ships of lighthouses
let's also make mirrors
for compassion and for love

and not-mirrors for
movement and equanimity

they are made we
make them in that
order

what you gave me

patience.   *a stone*

a small heart shaped pebble

metamorphic infill

patience is a stone worn in the heart

of an oyster's knowing grit

fine grained quartz stained by gobbelite

stained and fine grained

sitting in the stream of geology

patience.   a stone

spell for the untimely dead

the small & the wild
the undisclosed & the overlooked

the curlew pulling the rain along

the dust that the saw brings forth
the unwavering & patient line of the saw

you are seen

first naming of the island birds

hammer of daybreak

busy gleaner of the woodland floor

field walker   dung turner

tight wound spring

wind singer   wind bringer

sleeper in the sweet cress stream

breaker of dreams

murmurer of constant wonders

little ruler of the tides

scriber of sky circles

stretcher of pinions

broody hatcher of sea stones

threader of sea to shore

throat stretcher

half rung water ring

sudden singer at the suck of tide

little stander on water

sky swarmer   flier in shoals

walker of rock shadow

the island in September

yellow sea-cabbage   blue of scabious

white of yarrow   pink of yarrow

the eye of ragwort   sound of the harebell

cloud of meadow sweet   willowherb seed froth

salt in the mayweed   mayweed in sand

rust of docken   seared burdock

fruit of the bramble   splash yellow of lichen

bistort alone

long drift of chamomile   tormentil yellow

red of haws   red of rowan

bistort alone   bittersweet

violet of self-heal   blue of scabious

black hips of the burnet rose you showed me

from: **synchronicities**

we nearly did a deal on the mare & her foal at foot   after haymaking
rain starting   Tim O'Sullivan drove off on his cabless tractor
of course he took my old duffel coat for its hood
in the tractor shed a wren built her nest in the coat pocket
& the following summer ripening   Tim rode across the bog to
        return it
nest   eggs   chicks   how could he disturb her

thirty years & five floors up   on the balcony in the pot with a
        clump of fern
a city pigeon has laid two alabaster eggs on a small clutching of red &
yellow cut electrical wires
& I cannot go out there   even for soft spring rain

three hundred years ago the poet Basho was walking steadily north
from the capital   pausing at Sendai he met the painter Kaemon
when they parted the artist gave the poet a pair of sandals   a
useful gift for a walker   laces dyed that exact & unfathomed blue
       of an iris
about which Basho makes a poem

reading the poem   I walk from my house under blown cloud to the
Botanic Gardens   passing where Muslim sells flowers
in a tub he has iris for sale the precise colour of Basho's laces
I greet Muslim & for less than the price of a loaf buy ten violet flags
equal parts bruised cloud & sunshaft

**sometimes the weight is equal to the weight of stars & the
    setting sun**

suns outlining cumulus and red falling ripe into the horizon

how the might have been moon eats our lives & love falls to its knees

blood on our heads an old landscape littered with haybales

& the long haze of applewood smoke from someone else's childhood

we are mortal   love is the bell of awakening

gentle us, hunter, our blood the exquisite gestures displaced

even elegant mind is clinging   who said mind is elegant
especially elegant mind is clinging   shadow left unsaid   sad heart
clinging   noonshadow clinging   elegant mind left unsaid   is
elegant clinging   unsaid mind is elegant   is no less in elegance

midnight sitting at the Carbeth oak
mind no less branched elegant

A belated & random birthday greeting for Bob on his birthday which should have been sent on July 29th (four years ago, when I procrastinated because I couldn't work the tune *76 Trombones* into a poem) & again this year Hobby Bobday (procrastinated, that is, in the face of so many others) & wanting to thank him for all those years of pure poetry.
10,000 years!   Stupa Day, 3rd August 2000

the course skandhas

listen form differ perceptions

hear emptiness defiled therefore

nor no form mind consciousness

them suffering suffering

because for liberating perfect right

therefore a mantra truth

proclaimed

gate

a valentine for Morven

of roses, yes &
hyacinths & amaryllis
all the forget-me-nots &
snowdrops as well as
stolen fruits

this is the fifth
the fifth fourteenth
of the one thousand
nine hundred &
forty four days

eighteen or so
million
heart beats
seeding significance
only to a man in love

who else counts
as growing plants
each shared
passing second
impermanent, perfect

discussing herons

1

which morning was it   that or this
you cooked deceivers & honey fungus   slippery jack & penny bun
larch bolete & boletus impolitus for which we have no name

while octobering trees gave their roof-dripping sermons
& parliaments & assemblies of crows & gulls
were whirring & kraaing   whistling & hooting

flighting together & shoaling with starlings
wheeling & rowing from ground to branch
branch to branch food in beak   denying   arguing

discussing   refuting   engaged in monkish discourse
& all so busy in the air   a great cacophony
rattling & belling the passing of the day

only the heron straight through this
silent but for wiping sky with her great greycloth wings
neck hunched   waved in time for which we also have no name

but in the evening   by Craigallian loch
a broken trout on the broad path   stiff
amid an explosion of scales of shining purpose

2

before the heron can appear on a river

the river must hold the possibility of a heron

a glimpse of a rose or rose hip

flash of goldcrest or echo of her call

lip roll of water backing against current

the possibility of water or air, unlikely elements

before the heron can appear

there must be a heron shape

dropped into the well of brain

after image of light flash

the river must not rise too high

or the heron will not arrive

when the heron comes to the river

an island appears at her feet

3

because I opened my eyes from sleep
the cormorant flew past the window

because I paused at the river bank
a kingfisher skimmed upstream

because I sheltered in a holly grove
the rainbow grew in the east

because the kingfisher perched there
a holly branch leaned to the river

because the river flowed here
the cormorant arched under

the cormorant surfaced under
under the surface under

holly roots under
riverbed under

sleep under under
the dusty world

for Larry in the Western Infirmary 261104

what if your mind is blank

let's turn the light around together

let's make tea at the hut

let's walk slowly along the riverbank

where the heron flies

where this morning that colour

I can't describe   radiant

iridescence of the kingfisher

flashed past borne by the bird herself

what if your mind is blank

let's sit awhile

the hardest thing

before moving again empty

through solid space

let's inspect amethyst mushrooms

shield bugs, thoughts

let's approve the world, simply

where passion takes us

what can be read into a thing

into the little finger size lizard lifted off the bonfire   its run the curve of my spine

into gnats pouring themselves incessantly into a vessel of air that never moves

into mallard becoming riverflow   into finches sowing seeds of the seen   into crow become sound become ear

into the weight of balsam scent in September become air that is smelled   into the man singing whose throat opens & Kelvin riverbed syllables flow

but   bursting   that it happens?

in the vessels of the heart   in the choice of aorta this minute or if you will a suspicion that

there is more   that someone has more & will steal more   when there is no more   when it has moved on

hovering kestrel as air   thunderhead as water   water as emptiness drinking the soil which is clover   as calcium   as bone which is looming stormcloud   this is that   this is

that junky neighbour from no.15 chapping the door at 3am looking for tinfoil

16 broken bottles of Buckfast   Saturday night   Cedar Street & North Woodside Road

no. 17 neighbour   dead for days   only his decaying smell bringing forensic police in white paper overalls

Johnboy 20   knifed & dying in Grovepark Street   lifespan
length of dream   night churning

what can be said of a thing with clarity

that this is that   where this rain stitches that river   we practice
being while dealing   where wet leaves of this tree brush heads

but back to front   upside down   sideways   stealing words we
cannot steal time

from the ogham

Cloghane Carhane
EQQEGGNI MAQI MAQI CARRATTIN

was he a friend

women fight

here among the ivy

now I begin to see him   lust

           in the ivy

women fighting

bees swarming

now we're all angry

should be

           taking stock

           minding cattle

was he a friend

thief of the grove of silence

his lust

drains blood

boils my blood

was he a friend

Cloghane Carhane

underneath his name

carpenter's work

it starts to make sense
hazel
it starts to make sense
alder
the most withered wood

the job in hand

clarity

cutting

the highest of bushes
ivy
nettles
the most withered wood

it answers muster
the elm
the apple
forest & orchard
and the hazel

Poltalloch
CRONAN

there is a murmuring

such beauty

the rose redness that grows in a man's face

the intensest of blushes

    equally wounding

        sense comes to him when he goes to his death

the noise is made

the noise made in delirium

the noise made marveling

the noise is made

when he goes to his death sense

death enfolds him

a sheltering hind

Dunadd

the people of the boar will pass this way
& leave their print

above

      his vital force

      our ally

      our ally

      a destroying force

below

      from the earth

      his vital force

      the head   the emblem

      the back fit to break

      our ally

to the red face

the reddened face

to the fear white face

a force of freedom

Keiss Bay　　　　　(for Kate)
NEHTETRI

daughters of the four winds

no more sleep

liberation

makes friends

like a hound her pups

like coals to a fire

friends

like emptiness filled

three times

it fires the blood

it lasts forever

on the stone from the **Moor of Carden** *at Logie Elphinstone*
CALTCHU

the disc & lightning   new moon & cunt   disc   lightning & wheel

thirty cattle welcome the shade

                    (they're hot)

sixty cattle welcome the shade

                    (they're thirsty)

cows   strippers   heifers   yearlings   stirks   welcome the shade

                they welcome the shade of the fairest tree

dappled light on the brindled cows

delights the eye

this is for the growing of plants of stalks of stems of boles of trees

my eye is delighted

by dappled brindled cows

                in oak tree shade

cows   heifers   stirks   calves   in shade

thirty head

sixty head

fine beasts

fine tree

the yew wound with ivy   **Gigha**
VICULA MAQ CUGINI

the old man speaks

                     nothing.   *fires gone*

       shrivelled old wood

                         no life.   *no zip of bees at the hive mouth*

                  cold houses   *the moss grows*

                    my shame   *my pain*

                           dying   *an effort*

                      my pain   *the light*

                     no bustle   *no spark*

                         no life.   *no bees*

                  cold houses   *moss*

nothing sweeter than grasses   *ivy*

          shrivelled old wood

                        no rest   *no sap*

          shrunken old wood

Inverurie tree felling   (for Colin MacLeod on the M77 route)

the ninth one   the bleeding yew of Brynach   period storms

the oldest wood

in the oldest wood

                brings blood from sap

                brings mouth corner mutterings

the brought blood hot as coals

                begins answering

                side mouthing the logging

fraught as menstrual blood

                begins blitz & serpent mouthing

                of sap and blood

& the allies of wood

cut off a breast and fight

& death

busy as a bee

Abernethy

QMI

      quick   gentle

    so hard to quell

           elder

the hind   the hunt

       quenched

         elder

Ty'n y Wlad, Crickhowell (for Graham & Ursula)
TURPILI MOSAC TRALLONI

curses developers & keens wild land

unsung
        rivers   hills   woods

in stone houses
red faced at the fire   burning
the sweetest of wood from
the veteran woods   eye's delight

it's not the beginning of an answer
        even the strongest of effort
              burning after slashing
                    ploughs behind horses
it's not the beginning of an answer
        busy   busy
it doesn't begin to answer

there was stillness
        bath   food   fire

damn the herdsmen & red faced farmers

how smoothly the woods are gone
              sweet hag woods
                  apples of my eye
                      my darlings

Shetland tree stories (for Alec Finlay)

Cunningsburgh

1

oak alder elder rowan

the highest bush is only carpenters' work

what is safe for cows hides butchers

the highest bush is only carpenters' work

it's no use blustering

bright eyes look out for cattle

2

aspen hawthorn holly hazel furze ash vine & elder

dear distinguished trembling friends

wolves slink behind bush & tree

three times we'll burn them

wolves   tree & bush

cracking straight sweet limbs & nut & seed

become axle-tree

become stick

become poison

become axle & spoke

become blood

Gurness Broch
INEITTEMEN MATS   *TEMENOS*

last becomes first in ash womb   this place is for women

inside yew   a given thing to daughters

aspen trembling   this place is for nieces

reddest fruit of her female she holly

briar's holding   sanctuary for grandmothers

wind silvered fir   set apart for the crone

willow sap source   home to quean

all blood moon gathered

the unbreathing paid for with breathing things

from **Stroke Mother**

to turn the stone of sorrow to song

shall I say a prayer for you before your death

a novena that you might not know the night yet

the calculations of karma before

an unkaddish of unknown praise untold

a mantra for your motherhood

let me count beads

let me count the little mothers (since I am grown big)

let me count the big mothers (of childhood)

let me lie and say that love destroys death

but I do not believe

                        it is said
                        there is a human flowering

from the genitals through the coccyx & backbone to the brain
from the genitals through the belly & navel   through the pit of
        the stomach
the chest & throat to the brain
from both sides of the navel circling the belly
from the genitals between the coccyx & backbone between
        the belly & navel
& the pit of the stomach to the heart
the outer arms link the shoulders with the palms through the
        middle fingers
the inside of the arms link the palms with the chest
from the soles through the outer ankles & legs to the genitals
from the soles through the inner ankles & legs to the genitals

                                  small mother lies in the bed

                to be aware of the line
                the line of affirmation
                the driven line

the base of the spine   /   the world wheel
the navel   /   fire
the heart (full) the throat (thick)   /   air & sound
between the eyes
the crown
& above

                with air and with sound
                we grieve
                with full heart and throat
                through the line of photographs
                on the chest

the world wheel & the navel   (mani   the jewel)

                        outside the window
                        the apples ripen slowly
                        there is a profusion of web
                                making spiders
                        unripe hazels drop in the gutter

the word we are here to discuss

                        I cannot say

                        mother agrees
                        everybody's memory is trailing away
                        mother says
                        long   discursive spiralling & looping
                        the line continues

it is said
there is a human flowering

                        it is trailing away

there's no dissembling before death
    she's deaf
she hears the meaning of words under words
impassive to lies and excuses

    she is at the centre of the web

much as the spider whose silk still
    in memory spans that littoral path
she is beautiful as sun in the water on her own web
when there is nothing more
    than spaces between
silk strands between
    supporting grasses which are
just grasses

we call this love
we call this life
        she says it is death
    death says it is
        becoming death

death becomes death
    & we live

    necessary absence

Good Friday 280397 10 christians walking down Gibson street the first 2 carrying a life sized wooden cross; that is, one big enough for a crucifixion. They are flanked by 4 policemen. Who do they need protection from? Is it we who need protection from their millennial solemn bell-laden evangelism? 85 today. I remember the Rembrandt *Carcass of an Ox*. There she is in the background

the men with their knives
& aprons are gone
basins of blood carried
head skin hooves

flayed   gutted   the
carcass hangs
from a pole
from hooks in the darkness

I remember her infinity shaped
rubber kneeling pad
unused now she
bends her back no longer young

scrubbing slaughter
from the flagstones
who taketh away

thinking stupawards, heaven approaches

a kind of keening, a kind of kaddish, a kind of truth

nothing, of course – am I alone in remembering d.a. levy
– another dead & gone buddhist jewish visionary – something like
logic pulses between my shoulder-blades – between my wing-
stumps – not that I not-believe in heaven, you know – death, of
course, nothing, of course – & mother is gone – this her farewell
among the sleeping & the dead – of my life, they all stare hard
– the dead, working stupawards – never ending, no hosannas
but this, this – this goodbye, eyelids clenched – when this is all
the proof I need – emptiness not empty – the last goodbye, the
deep farewell – the greeting of the bardo-gone – the welcome
into life, the recognition – the birth, and yes, hosanna – the start
of love, of being time – of sweet delusion & night-chill & this
my mother's gift – her love, my one void-awakening – my long
farewell, my sweet hello – night chills, the traffic surrs – love,
love, the last smile of gone, the last fading grin of goodbye – of
nunc dimmitis, of compos mentis – of that other hasid's hosanna
– I stand, spin this, down time, stupawards, stupawards – the
jewels within, the dream the body – stupawards, being time, the
real words, the deep century-long Hollywood goodbye – the
goodbye recognition, the nod sourceward – the love she showed,
unthinking, the real, the visionary words – the quotidian – the
love, the real goodbye, the singing love.

Through crackling air   each Sunday
        for twenty one years
                while women mouthed Hail Mary

and farm bachelors smoked Woodbines
        outside chapel doors
                I drove wet miles to the village phone

fed shillings
        then bright ten pence coins.
                We talked of time

and your grandchildren
        or the knitted socks in the post
                (which I wear still)

my small successes
        and my then manageable griefs.
                Now the phone rings out

or another might answer
        she no longer lives here
                (as if I could forget)

No longer here   but in
        twin graphs of memory
                lapse and sleep.

frost has killed
the last of your flowering
geraniums

as I watched

what is killing
me   that I watch

happen   mirrored
in the hall alone
I pursue lakes

flowing together

as ice & frost   & you
pattern my blood
to crystal

days shutter down
trees merely small plants

have printed your
name on the
rivers at source
they whisper
it & yell & shout
& fish mouth
it plankton
those shining
creatures light
a mirror to
the stars
one has cast my
prayer for you
in Brazil
one has thrown
my caution
in America
(& how these people
are the clouds)
silage wilts in
the rain grey
sky meadows
        – so patient
lungta –
meaning of Marie

in the Kelvin
by the Green Man
the newly
carved stupa

nothing is more
lightening
than a glimpse
of a meadow
through trees

what the island said

mountains and rivers are becoming realised beings

& close to Arran – my heart a salmon in my chest

soughing trees familiarity

at 5am woken by the men who have been eaten by gulls crying out in their agony

high beeches catch the bodhisattva's voice on the wind

bats swim in slow moving air waves

sudden click of sheep hoof on the shore below tidemark

fresh sibilance of the stiff brush sweeping barnacles from the jetty

soft drip of rain from leaf to drip leaf to softly flower yarrow

red of the poppies white of the chamomile stone of the wall generosity

solid sweet scent of bog myrtle

honey bees' nest in the dry bank

yellow stripe of the Burnet moth larva

that place of people where there is none

view of islands where there is no mainland   Antrim invisible

she lit his cigarettes from her mouth though she never smoked may she become the mountain   she is

Mullach Mor   I am

wake of the yacht on the swirl of light ocean on dark Atlantic

it does not shake   there are no tremors   it works

grasses nod *ash* they affirm *ash* and the spaces among

some of you went on the worn Caucasian rug that Barbara &
Ernst (more Hasids) gave in 1968
the one I sit on morning & evening

some of you was on the spoon I used to measure from the
green plastic crematorium urn labelled *this is it Kian* into a small
travelling brass nyasaland round box dated 1937   the year of your
daughter's birth

what could I do with the fine ash left on the spoon   not lick it like
honey from a jar   somehow disrespectful and to be honest you
probably wouldn't taste too good

so down the sink under tap water from Loch Katrine eventually
bound for the Clyde & open ocean   no doubt to mingle with
yourself again blown down from the height of Mullach Mor
where you also sit

    using your needles
           your thread
from your sewing basket
(& as I cd read this with your
                    magnifying glass)
thinking of your mother
                stroke /
tipping the last of the tea from the
packet into the caddy
opening the paper for the last
teafragrant
        leaf fragments
   stroke /
poems of daughters / solstice
recycling before that word
that word was thrift
that word was attention
the zen of daily life
before the z-word (stink)

on a day when winter's passed, waning moon, I carry Lawson's
Cypress, poplar, whitethorn to be stored & split for next winter's
fires

leaves caught in random winds appear as if birds taking flight
from the ground

taking two woodblocks I clap them together to draw attention
inform deer & buzzard & crow

I make five heaps of what's left of your ashes & spread one heap
to each newly planted maiden apple tree

the little wren knows it – ashes, trees, leaves – slowly, truly, form
& perception become mother-ground

understand love
mother daughter

lovers friends
children

as wind
love sifts your ashes

as hill
overlooks

as lochan rain
passes

as root
as word & wood

                  here to
                  sapling apples

                  let all who taste
                  know

                  whether hinds
                  that wander

                  or those
                  for whom planted

                  or strangers
                  you

                  in fruit
                  wood branch

word tree
together

Galloway Pippin
Coul Blush

Beauty of Moray
Thorle Pippin

Scotch Bridget
grand-daughters all

what a tight membrane
light is   light leaves
shadows of light
under leaves
against walls of light

I struggle between sleep
& wake & light
arrives with wind.
There is no other
sound   unless

it's trees mind flapping
Manjusri's flag in the
garden   where deer
according to their
own light move sound

lessly as of right
& light moves
you love &
on through

from the deer path to my door

here doing what I do best
weeding reading drinking

*

tax bills deadlines work undone
I plan a seat round the sycamore

*

time spent with black parrot queen of the night tulip
bulbs why not working sitting

*

early bus to town for teachings better
follow the drumming woodpecker into the woods

*

woodpecker drumming lapwings
wings lapping all the way

*

the marble hall all suits & security

guards missing the rain in my garden

*

old lady scattering bread for birds

blossom stuck to her shoes all there is

*

daughter gone into the world

sometimes I leave her room light on

*

autumn leaves gather in corners

doing nothing most gets done

*

old cooking pot under sky where I wash my hands gardening stir up

little frogs carry them to the pond where geese now argue no
$$\text{nothing}$$

*

fell over drunk precepts

gone vow gone shin hurts palm hurts instep hurts

⋆

such a small beetle passes so

easily across the written lines I labour over

⋆

stepping out for a piss I can't let the door

latch click listening to the owl's call

jottings

The poems in the book are, more or less, chronological.

The title **Printed on Water** was suggested to me by reading from the botanist & anthropologist Joseph Rock's notebook from his 1924 expedition to China & Tibet: (*verbatim*) "On our way down the river I noticed a lama with a board and rope sitting at the water's edge in front of him he had a stick placed erect while the board about 2 feet long and 8 inches wide lay flat in the water at the upper third of the board a cord was attached which the lama held in his left hand but the cord rested on the erect stick, he continually pulled on the cord across the stick just enough to lift the board a little out of the water and then let the board sink into the water again. We wondered what he was doing so we went down and inquired. He said he was printing images of buddhas but we said how was that possible. He then lifted the board out of the water and on the lower surface of the board there were attached five brass moulds such as are used in making the square earth cakes with rows of small buddhas. He was printing he said images of buddhas into the passing water of the Yellow River and thereby acquiring merit. It was the most astounding idiocy I have ever encountered. There he sat pulling the string for hours at a stretch letting the five moulds with buddha images sink into the water imagining that he was imprinting these images into the flowing water of the Yellow river. At his side he had a red cloth filled with barley, every now and then he took a handful of barley and threw it into the water, a grain of barley as offering to each little Buddha he imagined he imprinted into the flowing water thus sending thousands of imaginary water images of Buddha down the Yellow River with barley as offering. If that is not the height of absurdity for a grown man to occupy his time with such nonsense then there is really no such thing as absurdity. I took photos of him printing the images and then with the board out of the water showing the brass moulds."

In **Eitgal**, the joke about feet comes from *Folklore Studies Pamphlets 1: The Uglier Foot: An Anecdote In Old Icelandic Literature And Its*

Counterpart In Irish Folk Tradition; Bo Almqvist, Dublin 1975. The joke about monks on the island was told to me in a contemporary setting and was current at the time of writing. The *Annals of Innisfallen* record that in AD 823 "Skellig was plundered by the heathen and Eitgal was carried off and he died of hunger on their hands".

Ovid, in *Fasti* (introduction to Book 6), writes: "I will sing of facts but some will say I invented them". I take this as the starting point for **holy loch soap** which records the presence, between 1961 and 1991, in Cowal, Argyll, Scotland, of 5,000 United States nationals (service men & women & their families; sub-contractors and "servicing agents"). At Holy Loch, the US Navy operated and serviced nuclear submarines and their armed missiles.

During those years, between 75,000 and 150,000 US nationals passed through the town of Dunoon, on the shores of Holy Loch. The figures are vague, since for "security reasons" no accurate figures have ever been issued by either the US Navy or the MOD. As also there have never been precise figures on number and type of missiles present, accidents, or indeed what remains on the seabed, tangible or otherwise.

The town of Dunoon, with a population of some 9,000, was the scene of clashes of culture, nationality, sovereignty, territory, race and economics.

In 1987, I was trained as a "facilitator" on the US Navy Alcohol / Drug / Substance Abuse Program (my personal preferences are not the issue here) but felt drawn into the conspiracy where even facial hair (in men) was suspect; in effect a paranoid fifth columnist. I lived at that time in Glendaruel, a W Highland glen 20 miles from Dunoon over the hills.

*Accident: in November 1981 a Poseidon missile being winched between the tender and a submarine fell, or as the US Navy put it "descended at a faster than normal rate".

*Security: provided by 45 US Marines "who are not well known for their refined behaviour" armed with M16 rifles, pump action shotguns and stun grenades stood permanent guard behind the heavy steel doors of the nuclear storage area.

*Command: SSBNs (nuclear-powered attack submarine or 'hunter-killer') rested with US Navy's Commander-in-Chief Atlantic (CINCLANT) at Norfolk, Virginia, exercising control through Commander-in-Chief US Atlantic Fleet (CINCLANTFLT) and the Commander Submarine Force Atlantic Fleet *as part of the US strategic nuclear forces*. Under a 1961 agreement, 400 warheads, (two submarines worth) were allocated to NATO's Supreme Allied Commander Europe (SACEUR) who would use them as theatre weapons for 'deep interdiction missions against fixed targets'.

*Protest: the arrest of two trespassers from the peace camp at Sandbank (just outside Dunoon – and a US 'reservation') led to new fences and 24-hour patrols around the USS Hunley. When asked why this was necessary, one US Navy officer stated that while the protests might be peaceful at that time, "the PLO started out this way".
    The poem is not intended as a denigration of any individual (oh ?) but of a system and a foreign military presence in Scotland.
*Source: Malcolm Spaven in *Fortress Scotland*, himself quoting sources as varied as *The Scotsman* and US Congress, House Appropriations Committee.

A belated & random birthday greeting for Bob (Cobbing) is drawn from Thich Nhat Hahn's commentaries on the Prajnaparamita Heart Sutra; *gate* being the first two Sanskrit syllables of the mantra.

Ogham is the script used for inscriptions on stone during the 4th – 8th centuries, preserving the earliest known form of the Gaelic language. Of about thirty inscribed stones in Scotland (most are to be found in Ireland) some are on the west coast in Gaelic, while most are in the east on Pictish symbol stones in what is assumed to be a Pictish language. The versions are derived from the original inscriptions (or recorded transcriptions from RAS MacAlister in his *Corpus Inscriptionarum Insularum Celticarum*) and two "word oghams" from the Ogam Tract in the 14th century Book of Ballymote as recorded in Sean O'Boyle's book *Ogam: The Poets' Secret*.

In **Stroke Mother** the word *stupawards* belongs to dom silvester houédard. It appears in his poem *anacyclic poem with two shouts* ("written for the artists protest committee for their call from los angeles for a tower against the war", written in January 1966). Plus ça change . . .

the deer path to my door is literal; it leads to my wooden hut at Carbeth at the foot of the Campsie Fells.

Printed in the United Kingdom
by Lightning Source UK Ltd.
124422UK00001B/475-501/A